THE 13 BRITISH COLONIES IN THE UNITED STATES
US HISTORY FOR KIDS GRADE 3

Children's History Books

Speedy Publishing LLC
40 E. Main St. #1156
Newark, DE 19711
www.speedypublishing.com
Copyright 2017

All Rights reserved. No part of this book may be reproduced or used in any way or form or by any means whether electronic or mechanical, this means that you cannot record or photocopy any material ideas or tips that are provided in this book.

In this book, we're going to talk about the thirteen British colonies. So, let's get right to it!

Columbus Taking Possession

After Christopher Columbus sailed across the Atlantic Ocean and "discovered" the New World in 1492, the first settlers to come from Europe were from Spain and Portugal. There were already people living in the Americas. The Native American tribes were living in North America and there were many native peoples in South and Central America as well.

Eventually, the English began claiming land in North America. The first colony to be settled by English settlers was Virginia, which was established in 1607. Over time, there were thirteen colonies along the North American coast.

Battle of Spotsylvania

These colonies had a long history as part of the country of England, until they decided they wanted to be free and independent. They fought to gain their freedom and became the United States of America in 1776.

WHAT IS A COLONY?

A colony is an area of land that is governed by another country. In many cases, the country that controls the colony is geographically distant from the colony that it governs. In the New World, most colonies were settled by people who came from their "Old World" countries in Europe.

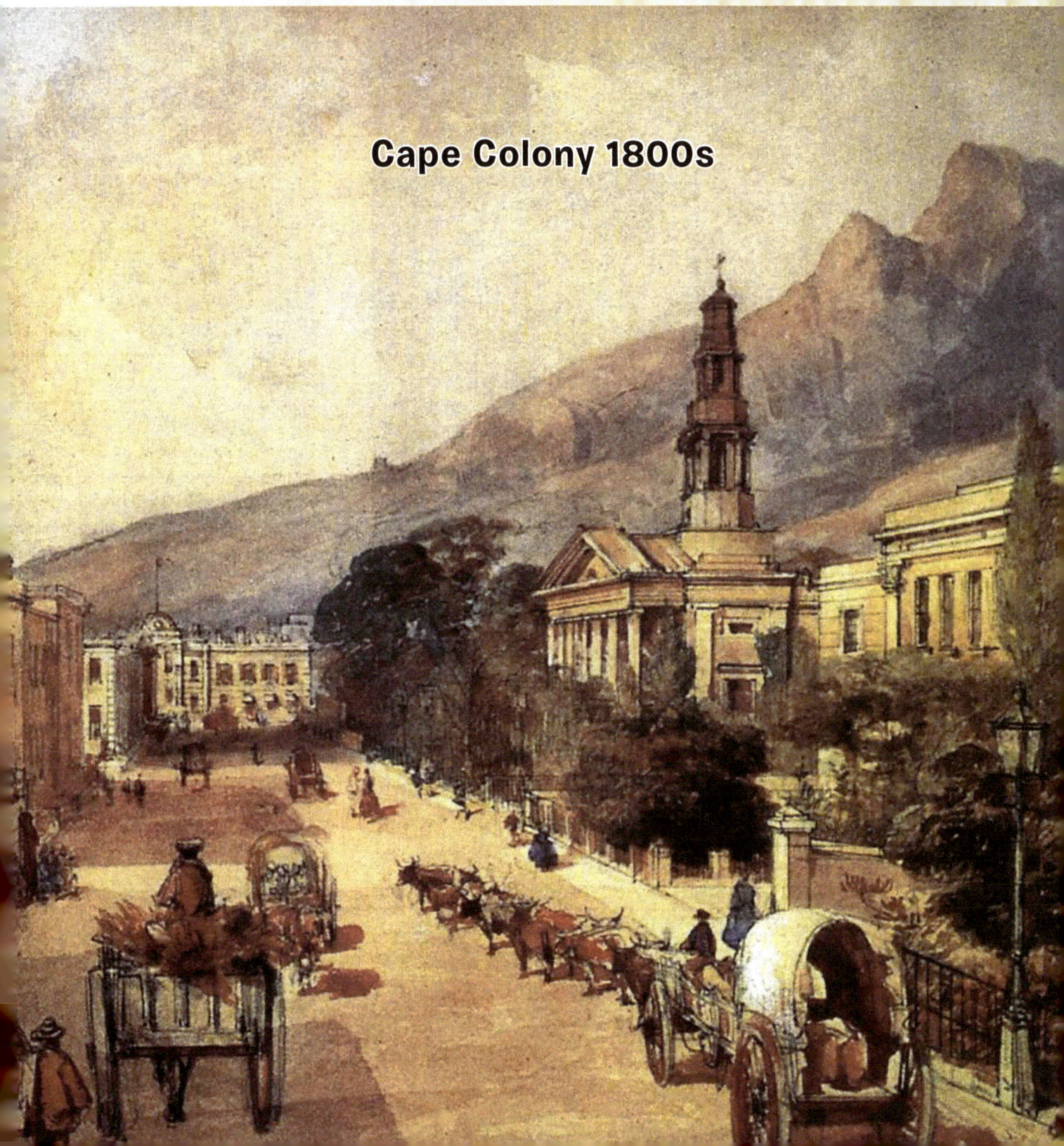

Daniel Boone escorting settlers through the Cumberland Gap

However, from the very beginning, America was a melting pot, which essentially means that many people from different lands wanted to settle there. Even though the British colonies were primarily settled by people who were citizens of England, settlers from all over Europe came to live in the thirteen British colonies.

ENGLAND IN THE 16TH CENTURY

During the 16th Century, the economy of England was in turmoil. The wealthy landowners had discovered that they could make more money from the sale of wool than from food. They were changing the farms into sheep pastures. Over time, less and less food was being produced, which led to a food shortage. Many farmers and agricultural workers were out of work as a result.

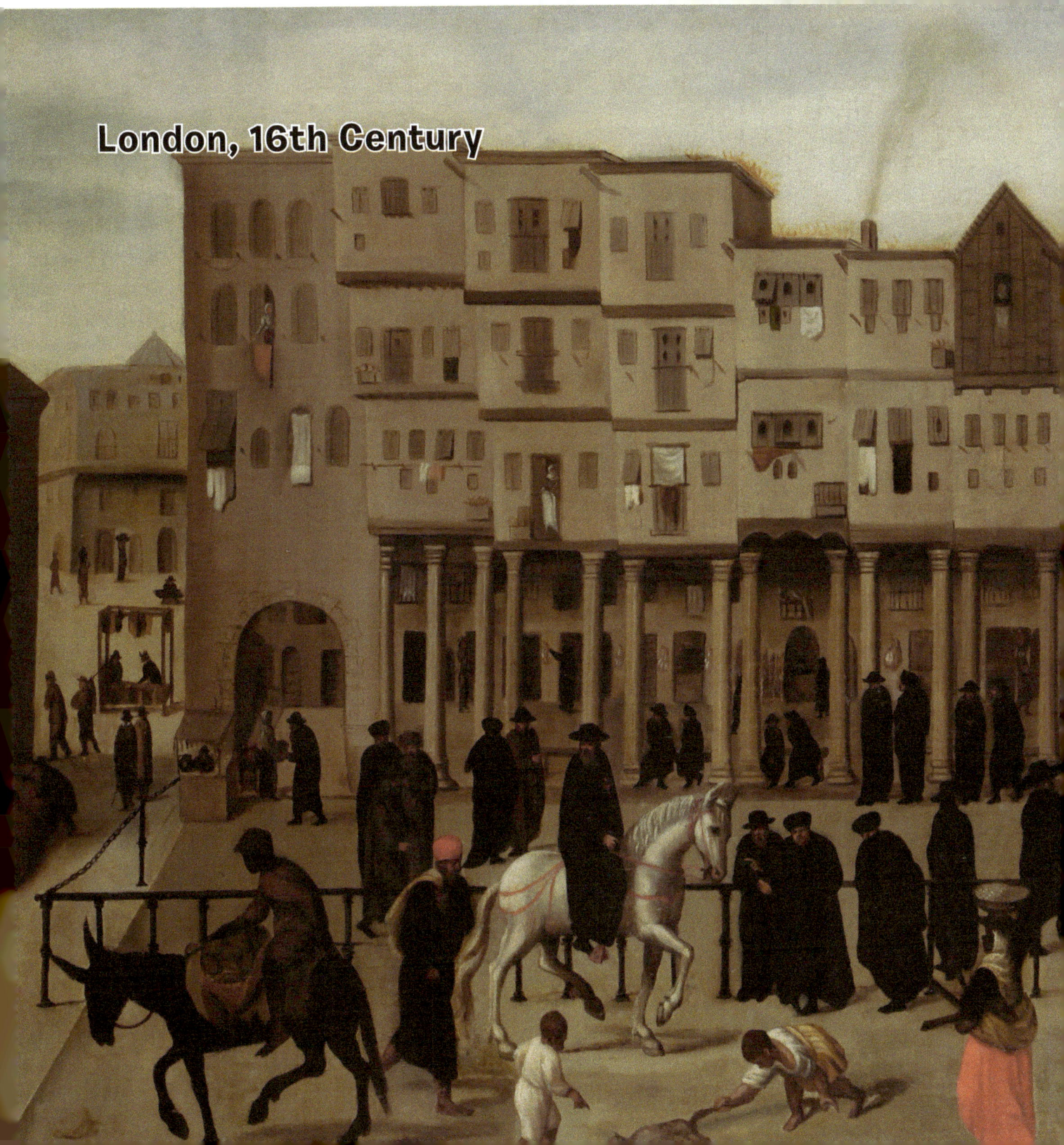

This was also the mercantilism age, which simply means that the European nations were pushing hard to obtain as many colonies as they could. At the beginning, the reason for venturing across the

dangerous ocean to the coast of North America was strictly for profit. Investors put their money into companies that they felt could make money for them in the New World.

WHY WERE THE COLONIES FOUNDED?

Queen Elizabeth was the monarch of England before the colonies were established. She was called the "Virgin Queen" because she had never married. She wanted to enlarge Britain's empire and become a more important world power than Spain.

Queen Elizabeth I

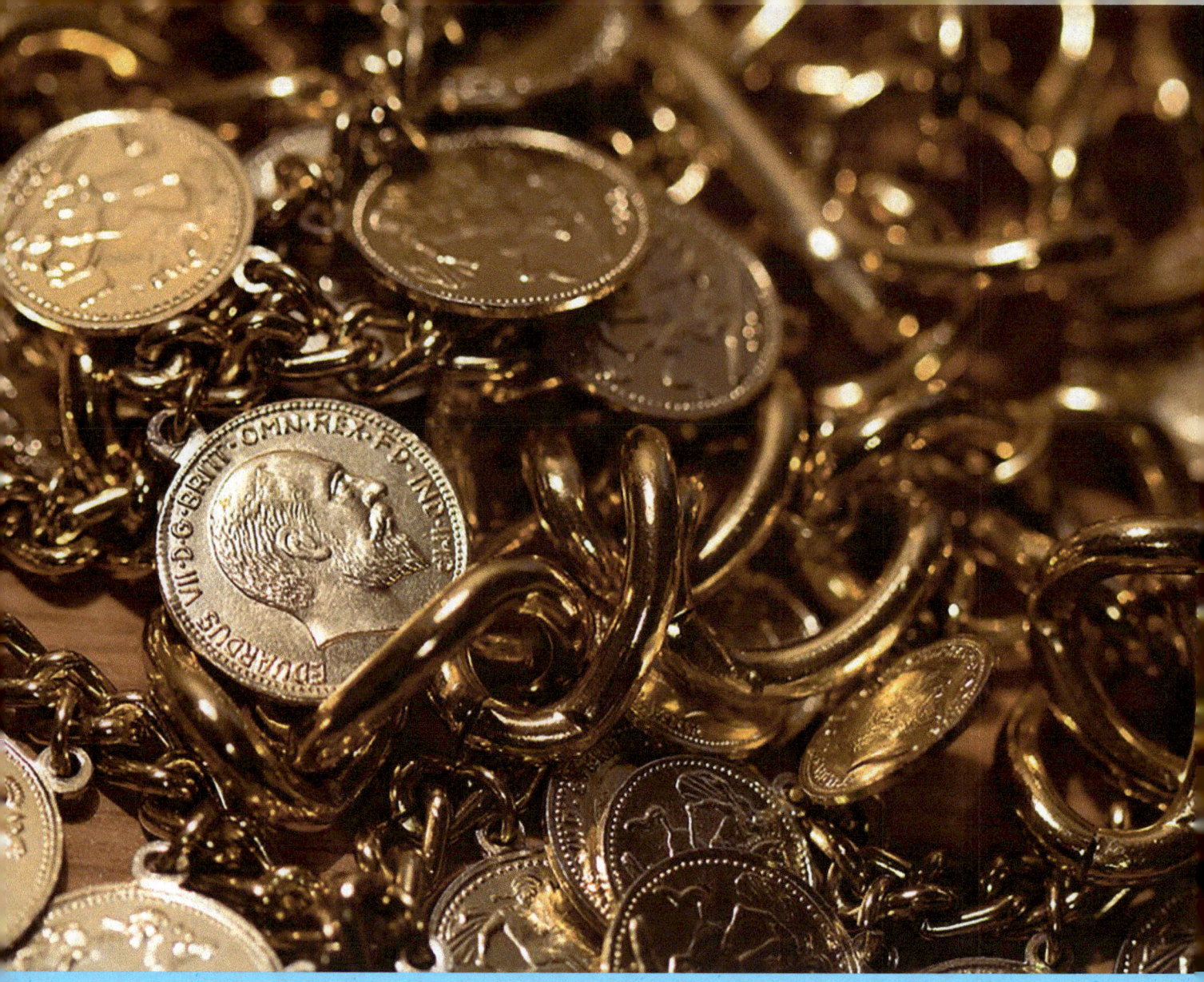

The British hoped to find wealth in the form of gold and silver in the New World. They also wanted to expand opportunities for new jobs.

The American coastline was valuable for setting up seaports for trading between the New World and Old World as well as with other countries.

After Queen Elizabeth died, King James I was the reigning monarch in England. He separated the lands of the Atlantic seaboard in 1606. He gave the northern half to the Plymouth Company to settle and develop. He gave the southern half to the London Company, which was later called the Virginia Company. The first English settlement that had been founded along the coast of North America had been attempted in 1587. This attempt became the famous Lost Colony of Roanoke. To this day, no one knows exactly what happened to the settlers who were there.

The First Day at Jamestown

A few months after King James I separated the lands, the London Company sent over 140 men to the lands known as Virginia. After several months, they arrived at Chesapeake Bay in the year 1607. They traveled up the James River and constructed a settlement there, which they named Jamestown after their king. At the beginning, the colonists were so occupied looking for gold to make a profit for the London Company that they didn't plan well on how to feed themselves.

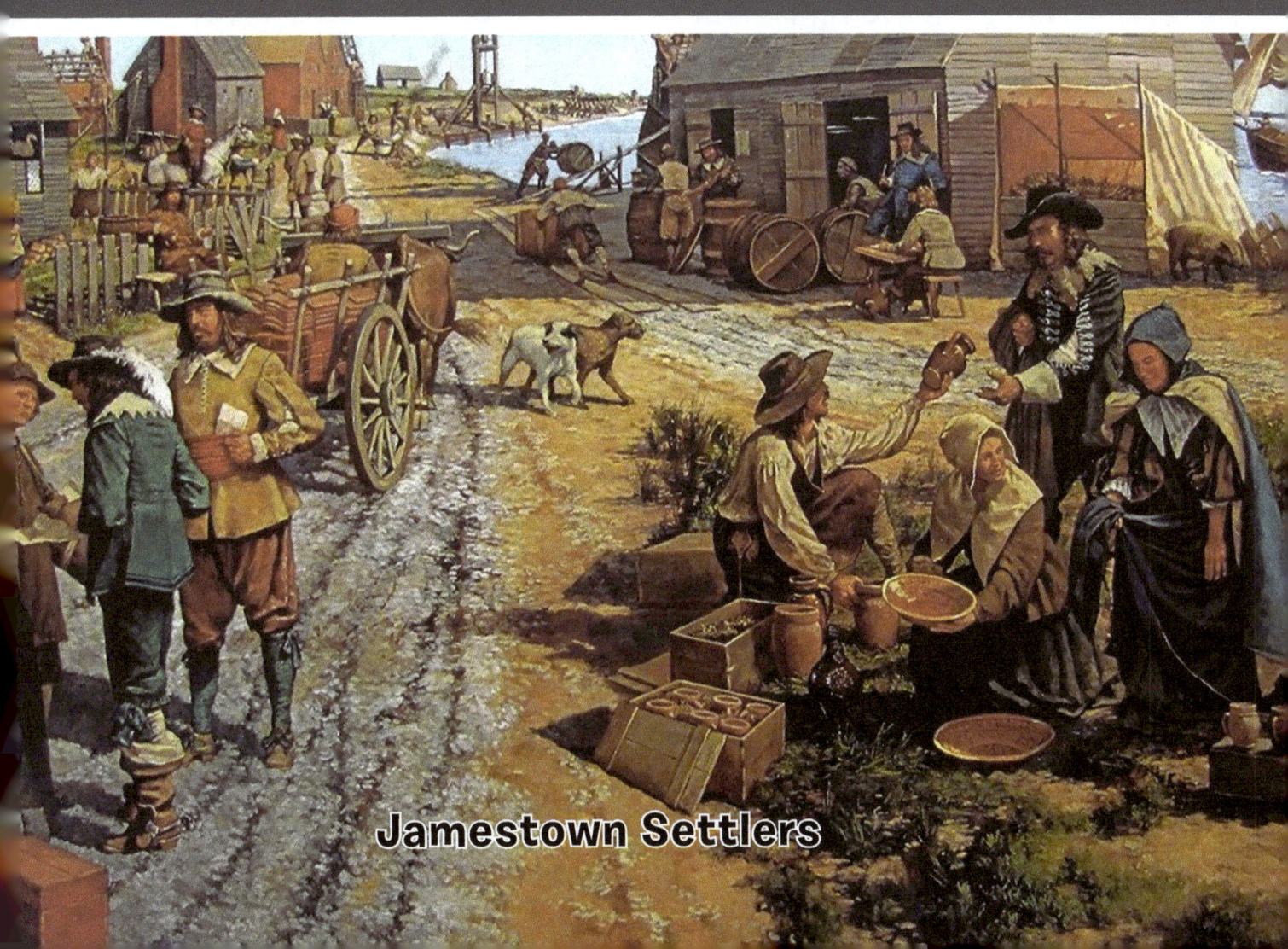

Jamestown Settlers

It wasn't until the settlers learned to make a profit from tobacco around 1616 that it seemed more certain that they would survive.

Slaves in Alexandria, Virginia

The first slaves from Africa arrived in 1619 to work the fields in the expanding tobacco industry. Eventually, Jamestown became the capital city of the Virginia Colony.

The remaining colonies weren't all founded at the same time. Each of the colonies had its own history. Some colonies were created so that their leaders and their families could practice their religion without the fear of persecution. Massachusetts was founded by the Puritans and Maryland was founded by the Roman Catholics. Both of these groups didn't want to follow the official religion of the Church of England so they were seeking religious freedom by coming to the Americas.

Mary Dyer was one of the Quaker martyrs who were persecuted for practicing their own faith in Colonial New England

There were also other reasons that certain colonies were founded. Some were primarily founded to obtain new opportunities for trade. Investors in England took great risks by placing their money into companies that were coming to the New World. Perhaps they didn't realize how difficult it would be to form a successful settlement in the New World.

England also claimed land and formed colonies to the north in what is now Canada. They settled Nova Scotia as well as Newfoundland.

THE THIRTEEN COLONIES

Here is a list of the thirteen colonies that became the first states of the United States in 1776.

- 1607, The Virginia Colony
- 1623, The New Hampshire Colony
- 1626, The New York Colony
- 1630, The Massachusetts Bay Colony
- 1633, The Maryland Colony
- 1636, The Connecticut Colony
- 1636, The Rhode Island Colony
- 1638, The Delaware Colony
- 1663, The North Carolina Colony
- 1663, The South Carolina Colony
- 1664, The New Jersey Colony
- 1681, The Pennsylvania Colony
- 1732, The Georgia Colony

1607, THE VIRGINIA COLONY

The London Company led by John Smith established the Virginia Colony and named it after the "Virgin Queen, Queen Elizabeth."

1623, THE NEW HAMPSHIRE COLONY

John Mason founded the colony and was the first to own land there. John Wheelwright later owned land there also.

New York Union Square

1626, THE NEW YORK COLONY

The Dutch originally established this colony, but the British took it over in 1664.

1630, THE MASSACHUSETTS BAY COLONY

Massachusetts was named after a group of Native Americans who lived in the area. The Puritan settlers who founded the Massachusetts Bay Colony were seeking religious freedom. Eventually, Plymouth Colony became part of the Massachusetts Bay Colony.

Puritan Settlers Arriving in Massachusetts Bay Colony

The Founding of Maryland

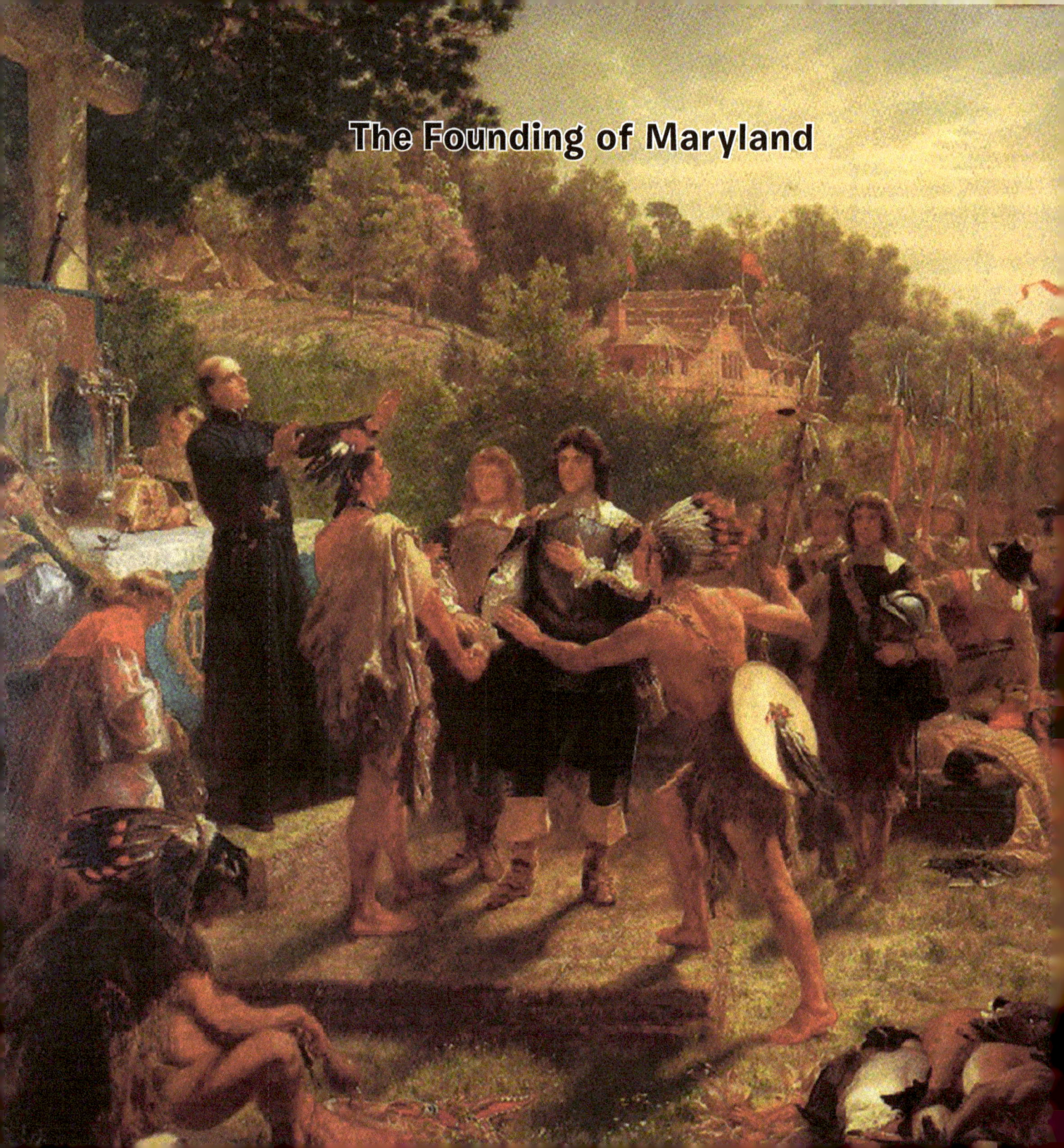

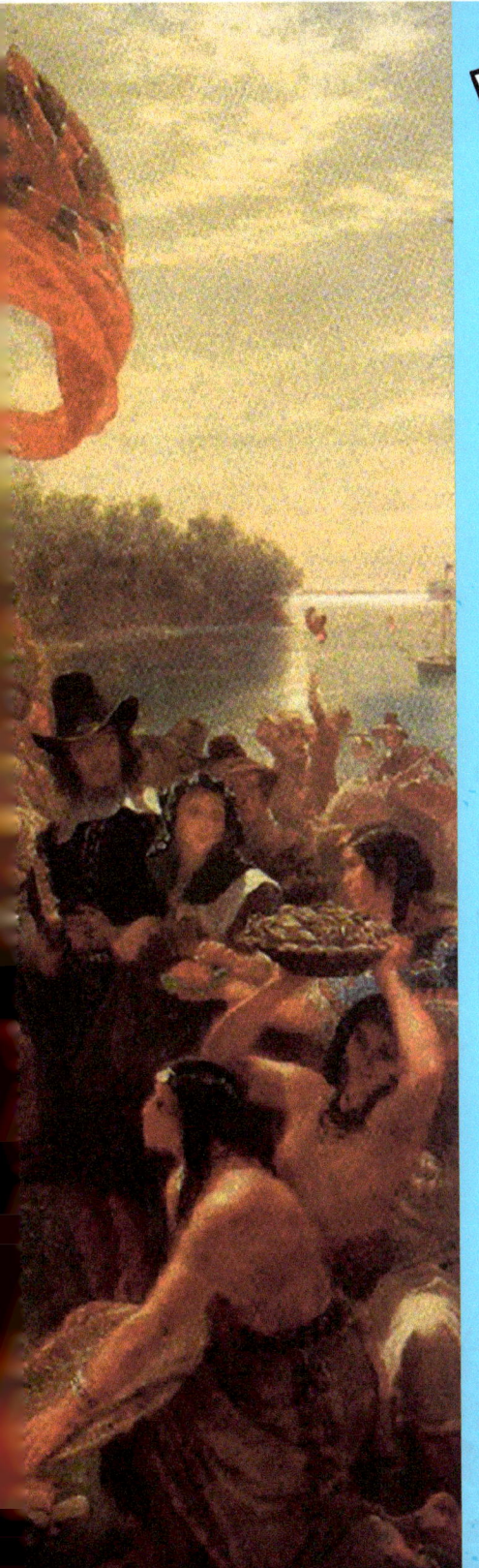

1633, THE MARYLAND COLONY

Maryland was named after Queen Henrietta Maria who was the wife of King Charles I. George Calvert and Cecil Calvert founded the colony to be a safe place for Roman Catholics to practice their religion.

1636, THE CONNECTICUT COLONY

Thomas Hooker was a Puritan who didn't agree with the practices of the Puritans in Massachusetts. He left the Massachusetts Bay Colony and started the Connecticut Colony.

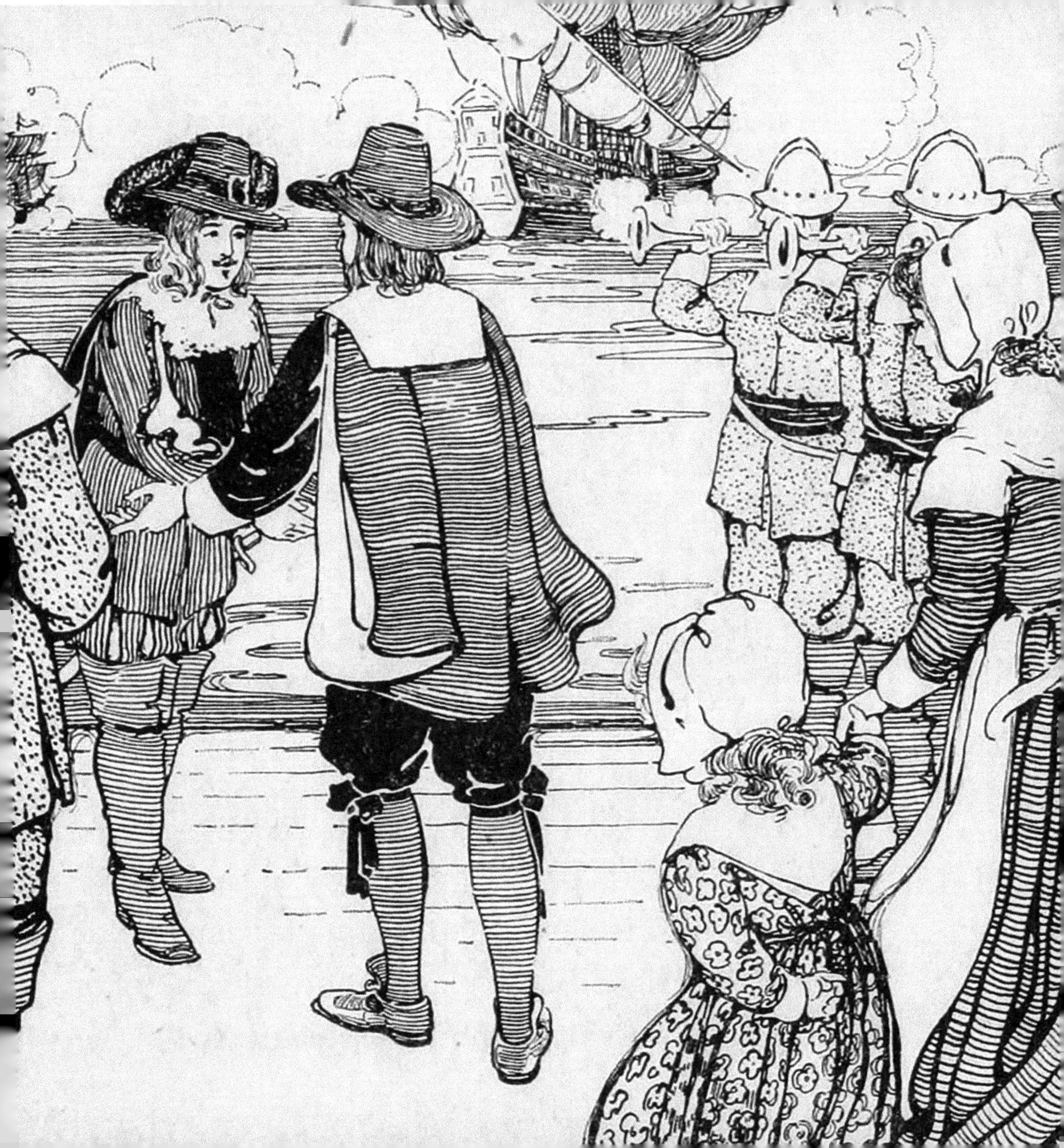

Return of Roger Williams

1636, THE RHODE ISLAND COLONY

Roger Williams established the Rhode Island Colony. It was designed as a place where anyone of any religion could worship without persecution.

Peter Minuit purchasing Manhattan

1638, THE DELAWARE COLONY

The New Sweden Company led by Peter Minuit established the Delaware Colony. The British claimed the colony in 1664.

1663, THE NORTH CAROLINA COLONY AND THE SOUTH CAROLINA COLONY

Both North and South Carolina were founded in 1663 and were named after King Charles I. They were also both part of the Carolina Province to begin with. In 1712, North and South Carolina were split into separate colonies.

King Charles I

1664, THE NEW JERSEY COLONY

The New Jersey colony was originally established by the Dutch. However, the British claimed it in 1664.

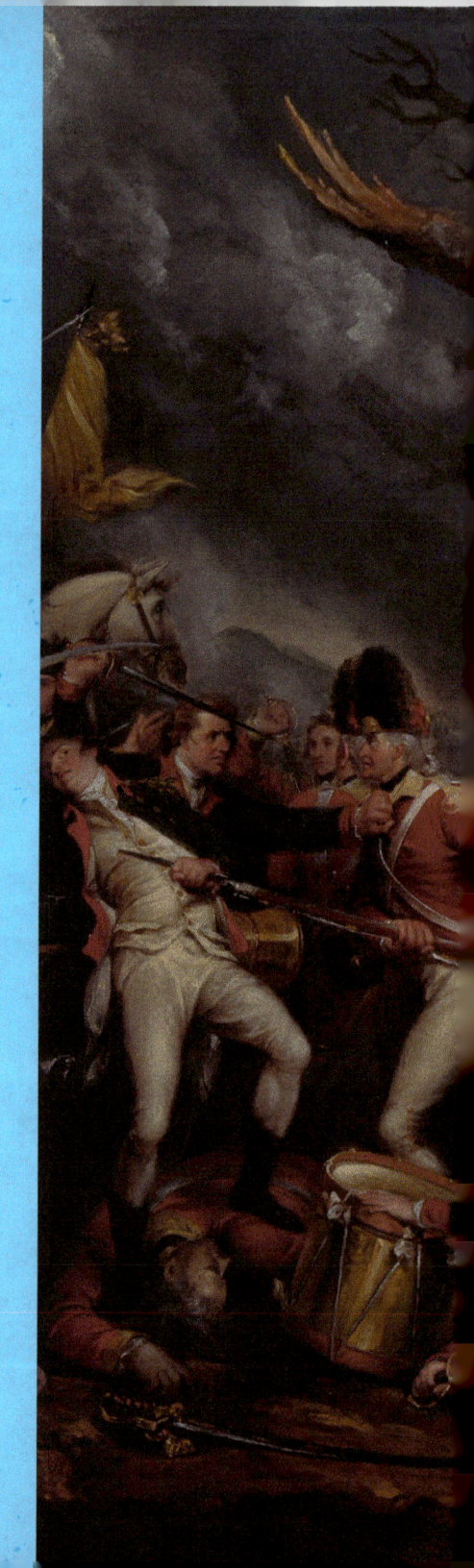

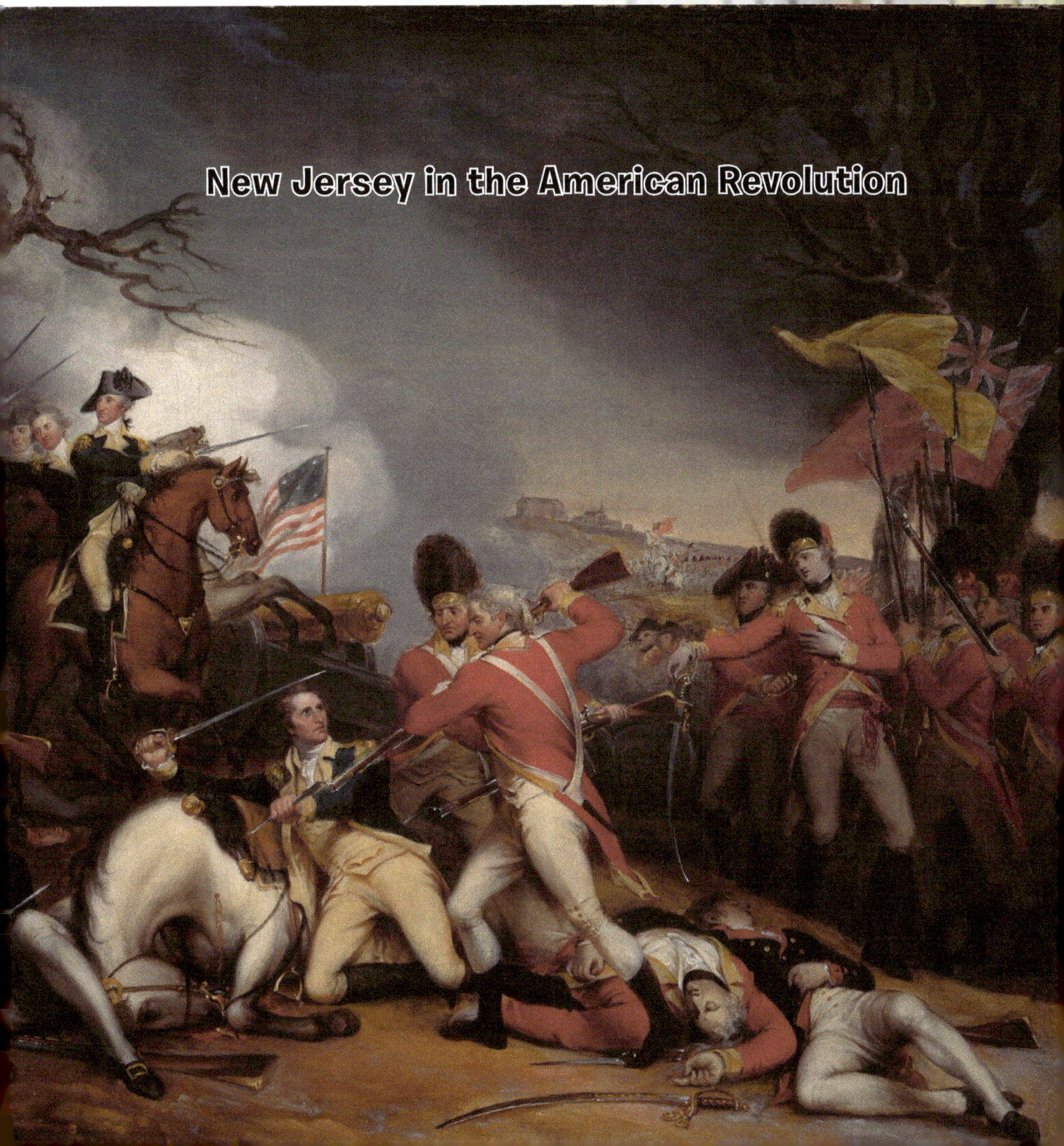

New Jersey in the American Revolution

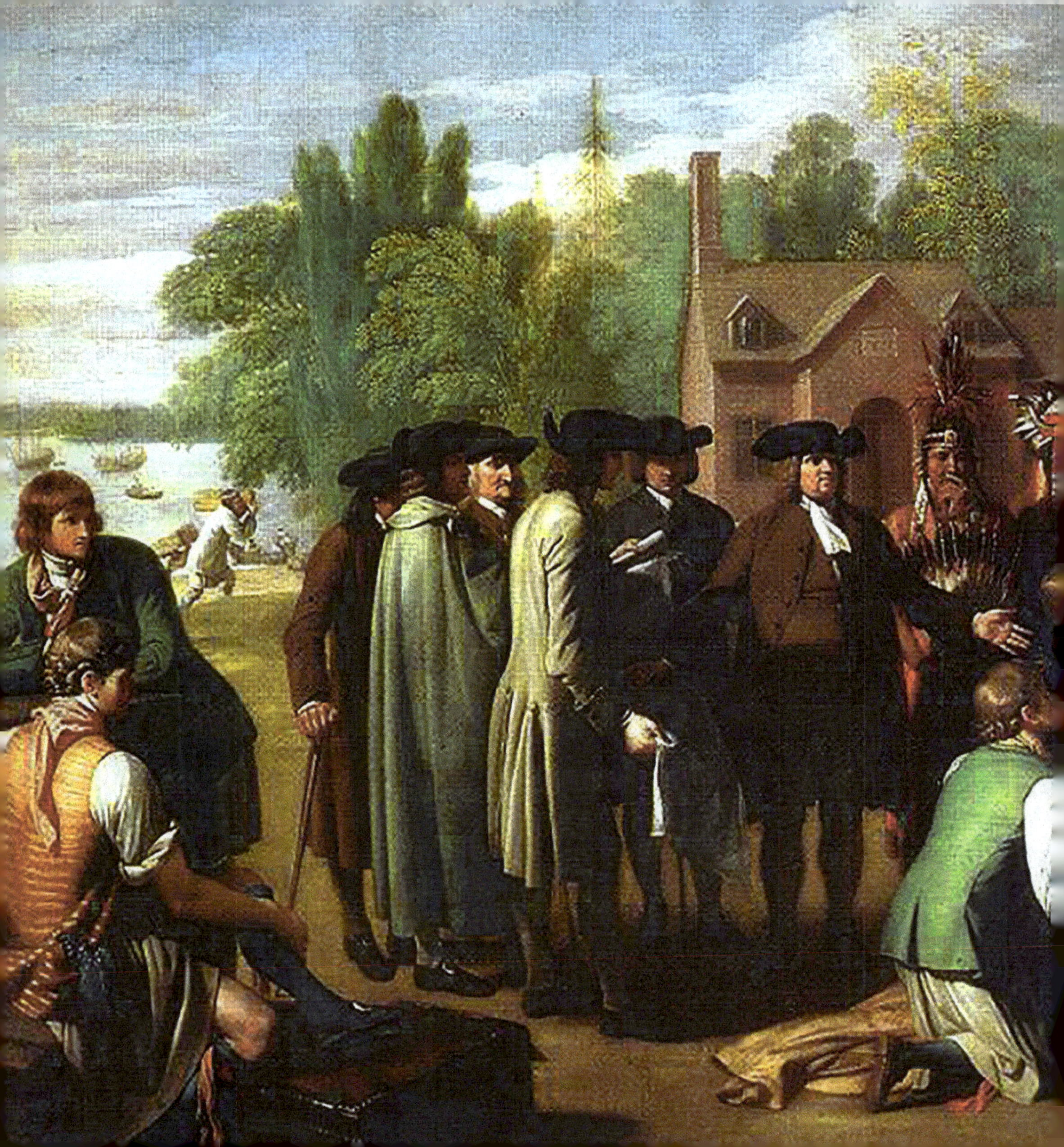

1681, THE PENNSYLVANIA COLONY

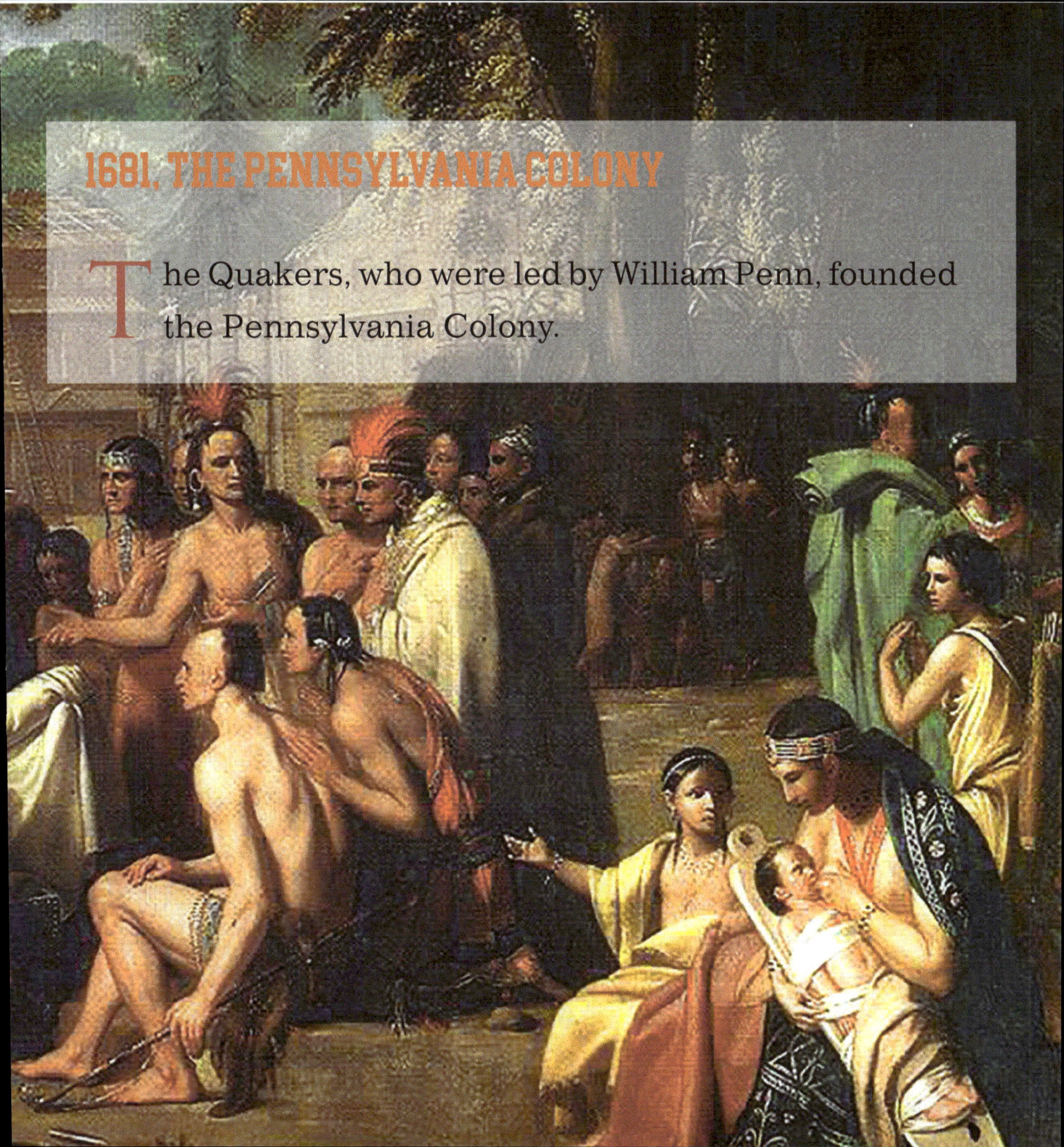

The Quakers, who were led by William Penn, founded the Pennsylvania Colony.

1732, THE GEORGIA COLONY

James Oglethorpe founded the Georgia Colony. The settlement was designed as a safe haven for people who were in debt.

Trustees of Georgian Colony

Colony Farm and Family in West Keene, New Hampshire

THE COLONIAL REGIONS

The colonies were grouped into three general regions: New England, Middle, and Southern Colonies.

There were four New England colonies: Rhode Island, Massachusetts Bay, Connecticut, and New Hampshire.

There were four Middle colonies: New York, New Jersey, Delaware, and Pennsylvania.

There were five Southern colonies: Virginia, Georgia, Maryland and the two Carolinas, North Carolina and South Carolina.

The Birth of Pennsylvania 1680

William Penn receiving Pennsylvania's Royal Charter from King Charles II of England.

Jamestown Settlers

FASCINATING FACTS ABOUT THE ORIGINAL THIRTEEN COLONIES

The original United States flag had one star and one stripe for each of the thirteen colonies.

Life in the New World was very harsh and unforgiving. At the Jamestown Colony in Virginia less than half of those that had come to the settlement survived the very first winter. The same was true at Plymouth Colony.

The Dutch originally populated the area that is now New York City. The city of New York was once called New Amsterdam and was governed by the Dutch colony called New Netherland.

The fall of New Amsterdam

Flags of United States of America

SUMMARY

After Spain and Portugal set up settlements in the New World, England decided that it should establish colonies as well. From 1607 to 1732, thirteen British colonies were established along the coast of North America. The founders of these colonies were frequently coming to America to obtain freedom of religion. Others were taking the dangerous journey across the Atlantic in order to get fame and fortune. After more than one hundred years of being ruled by the British, the colonies decided that they wanted the independence of their own country and the United States of America was born.

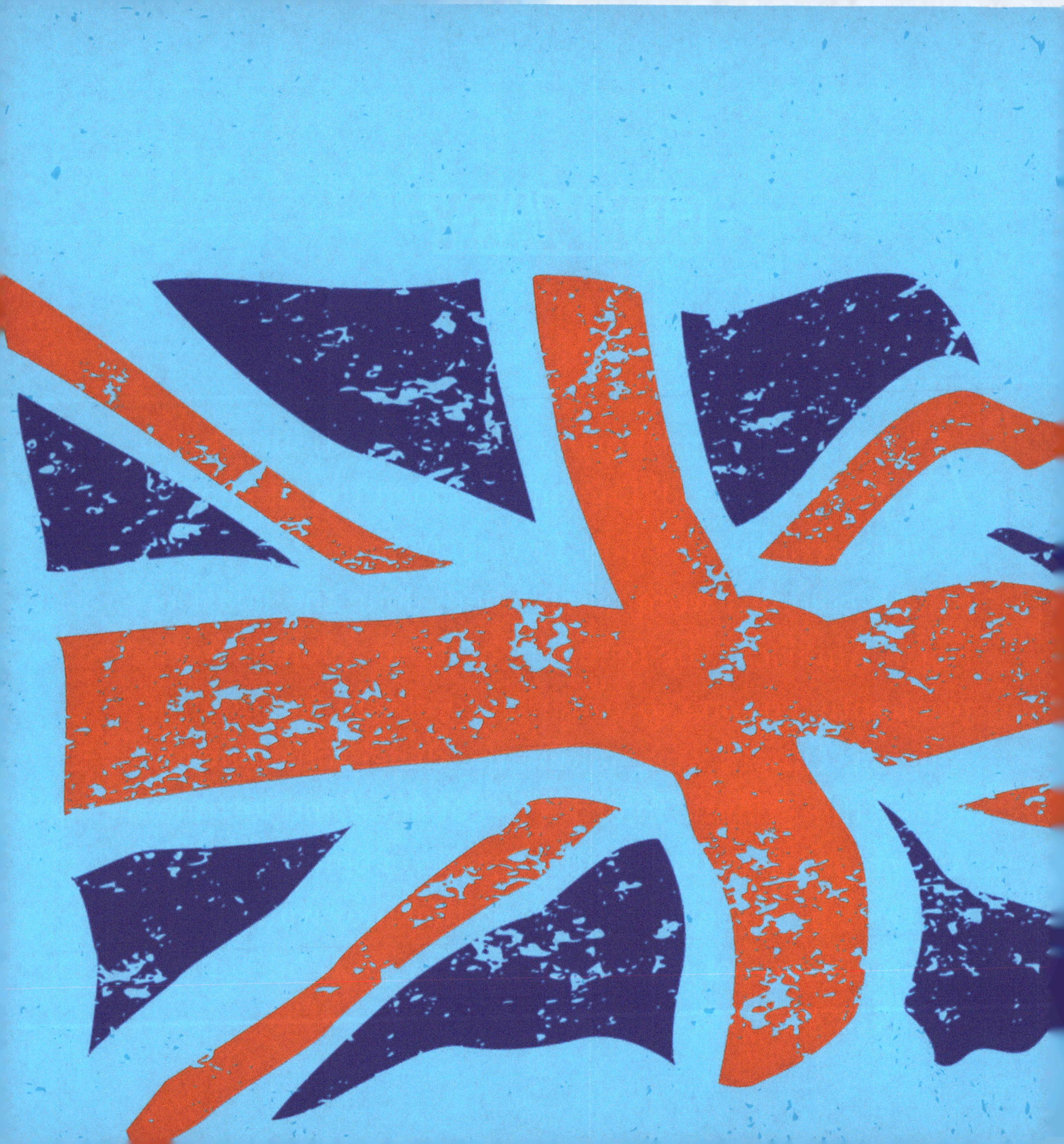

Awesome! Now that you know more about the thirteen British colonies you may want to find out more about the *Plymouth Colony in the Baby Professor book Who Created the Plymouth Colony? US History 3rd Grade.*

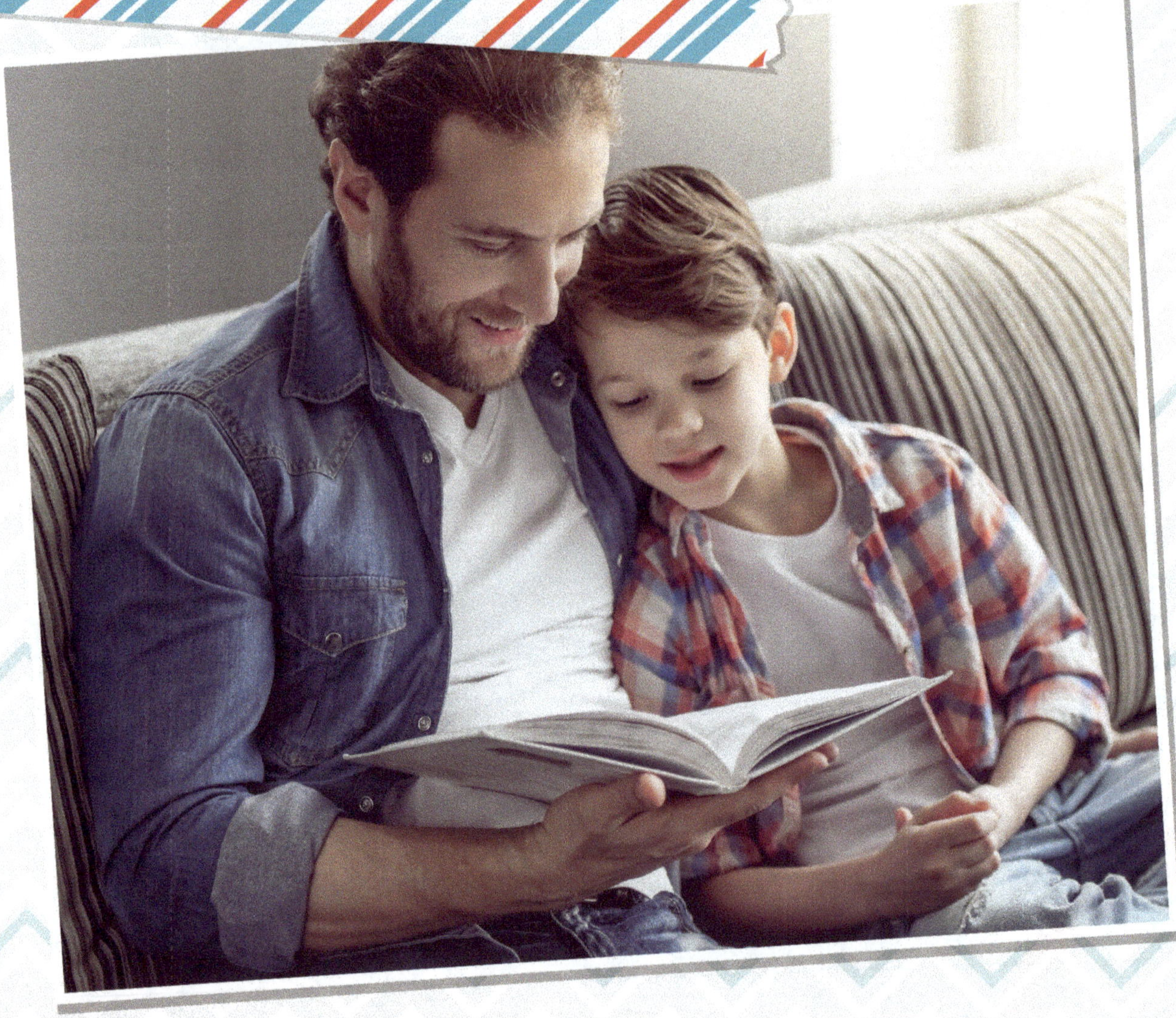

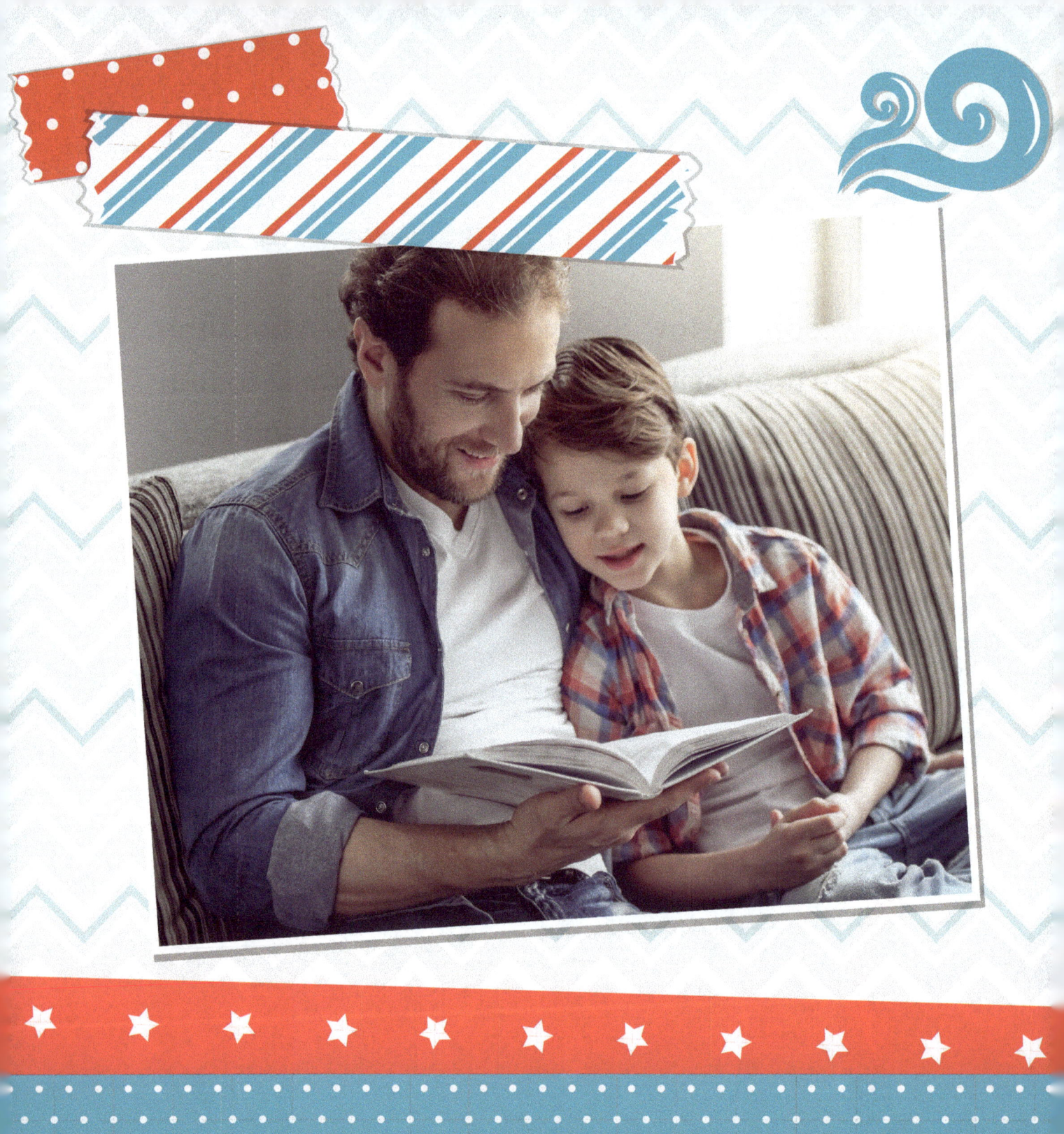

Visit

BABY PROFESSOR
EDUCATION KIDS

www.BabyProfessorBooks.com

to download Free Baby Professor eBooks
and view our catalog of new and exciting
Children's Books